I0884326

MADISON CHILDREN'S MUSEUM

CHANGING SPACES

Where Cows Jump over Moons . . .

JULIE KNUTSON

Cherry Lake Press

Published in the United States of America by Cherry Lake Publishing Group
Ann Arbor, Michigan
www.cherrylakepublishing.com

Reading Adviser: Marla Conn, MS, Ed., Literacy specialist, Read-Ability, Inc.
Photo Credits: © EQRoy/Shutterstock.com, cover, 1, 17; © Julie Knutson, 5, 6, 22, 27; © From the archive of Madison Children's Museum, 9, 25, 28; © michaeljung/Shutterstock.com, 10; © Everett Collection/Shutterstock.com, 13, 15; © SpeakingPics/Shutterstock.com, 16; © Travel_with_me/Shutterstock.com, 19; © BCFC/Shutterstock.com, 20

Copyright ©2021 by Cherry Lake Publishing Group
All rights reserved. No part of this book may be reproduced or utilized in any form or by any means without written permission from the publisher.

Cherry Lake Press is an imprint of Cherry Lake Publishing Group.

Library of Congress Cataloging-in-Publication Data
Names: Knutson, Julie, author.
Title: Madison Children's Museum / by Julie Knutson.
Description: Ann Arbor, Michigan : Cherry Lake Publishing, [2021]. | Series: Changing spaces | Includes index. | Audience: Grades 4-6. | Summary: "Learn more about how Madison's Children's Museum went from unwanted city block to dynamic children's museum. Explore the logistics of renovating the space and meet the people who made it happen. The book showcases a range of 21st century skills–from "Flexibility & Adaptation" to "Creativity & Innovation"–and shows how moving away from a teardown culture towards one of reuse helps tackle a host of critical challenges facing our planet and population. Thought-provoking questions and hands-on activities encourage the development of critical life skills and social emotional growth. Books in this series include table of contents, glossary of key words, index, author biography, sidebars, and infographics"–Provided by publisher.
Identifiers: LCCN 2020006352 (print) | LCCN 2020006353 (ebook) | ISBN 9781534168992 (hardcover) | ISBN 9781534170674 (paperback) | ISBN 9781534172517 (pdf) | ISBN 9781534174351 (ebook)
Subjects: LCSH: Madison Children's Museum–Juvenile literature. | Buildings–Remodeling for other use–Wisconsin–Madison–Juvenile literature. | Madison (Wis.)–Buildings, structures, etc.–Juvenile literature.
Classification: LCC AM101.M148 K68 2021 (print) | LCC AM101.M148 (ebook) | DDC 069.09775/83–dc23
LC record available at https://lccn.loc.gov/2020006352
LC ebook record available at https://lccn.loc.gov/2020006353

Cherry Lake Publishing Group would like to acknowledge the work of the Partnership for 21st Century Learning, a Network of Battelle for Kids. Please visit http://www.battelleforkids.org/networks/p21 for more information.

Printed in the United States of America
Corporate Graphics

With thanks to Brenda Baker of Madison Children's Museum

ABOUT THE AUTHOR

Julie Knutson is an author/educator fascinated by the endless ways in which people and communities can transform old spaces for new uses. She lives in Illinois with her husband, son, and extremely energetic border collie.

TABLE OF CONTENTS

Adaptive Reuse—More Than Meets the Eye

Essential Question: *What does the transformation of one city block reveal about the history of the place around it?*

It's a typical Saturday afternoon at the Madison Children's Museum in Wisconsin's capital city. Awestruck patrons watch as the museum's mascot, Gertrude the Cow, performs a task once reserved for nursery rhymes. She jumps over the moon!

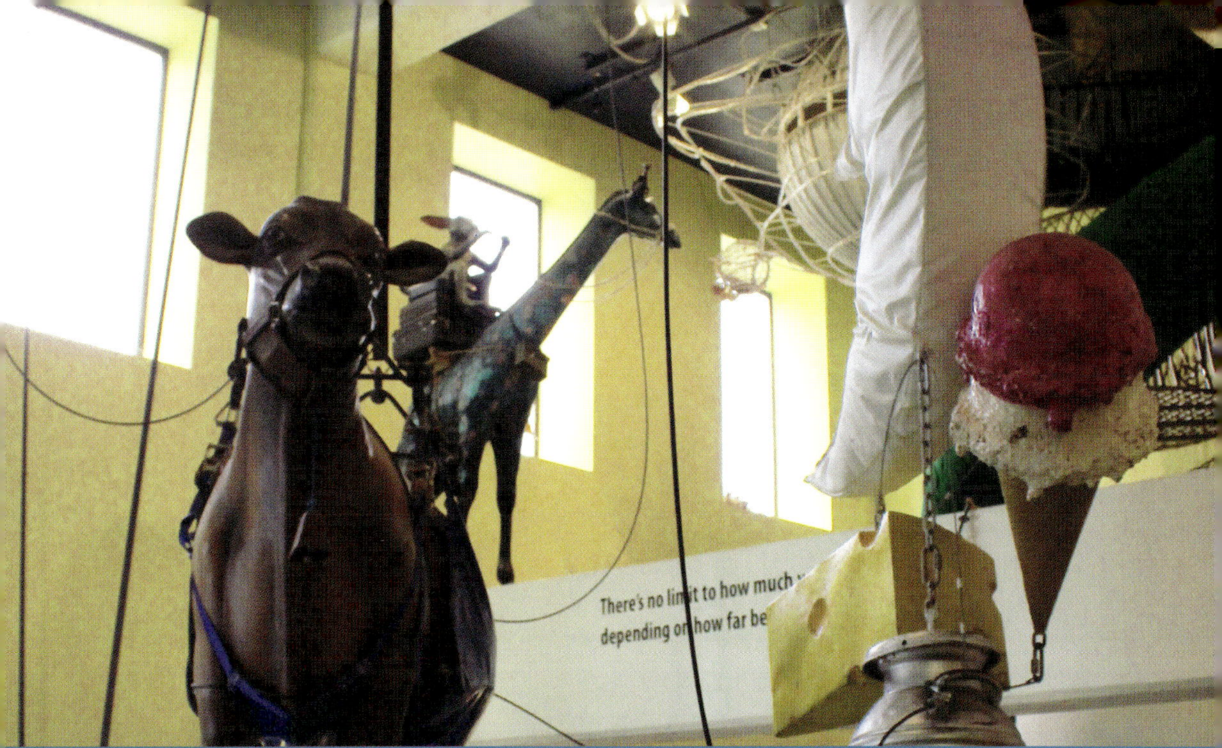

Gertrude the Cow is pulled skyward by a system of ropes and pulleys.

Gertrude is assisted by a team of youthful visitors, who hoist the fiberglass cow skyward with the help of a pulley system. Just a few steps away, a winded middle schooler treads in a human-powered hamster wheel. And one floor below, toddlers slide down logs and settle in for storytime in **yurts** with parents and grandparents.

The human hamster wheel at Madison Children's Museum has an energy meter that helps kids visualize energy creation.

When Did the Cow First Jump over the Moon?

"Hey diddle diddle,
The Cat and the Fiddle,
The Cow jump'd over the Moon,
The little dog laugh'd to see such Craft,
And the Fork ran away with the Spoon."

These lines first appeared in writing in a 1765 collection of Mother Goose's Nursery Rhymes. Some scholars trace the origins of the silly verses back even earlier. In the Medieval period, cats playing the fiddle were a popular image in **illuminated** *manuscripts.*

Occupants of this same space as recently as 10 years earlier wouldn't have imagined these sights and sounds. Throughout the 1920s and 1930s, it was a giant **retail** department store and customers browsed its floors for the latest fashions, housewares, and toys. From the 1940s until the 1970s, it was headquarters of the world's largest school, and military employees scurried about, planning **correspondence** courses. And in the 1990s and early 2000s, government workers researched and drafted laws within its walls. Throughout its history, this city block also hosted a church, private homes, one of the nation's first medical clinics, and a range of restaurants.

How has 100 North Hamilton Street come to have so many lives? What does this changing space reveal about the changing city around it? Who had the idea to transform an old department store into a children's museum? And what did it take to make this unique **adaptive reuse** project a reality?

CHAPTER 1

A Site with Many Lives

Madison—called "the City of Four Lakes" and "the Athens of the Midwest"—was established as the capital of the Wisconsin Territory in 1836. City planners then divided the land into 255 blocks. Block 99, where the Madison Children's Museum now stands, was a geometric oddball. Throughout its history, its quirky triangular shape required designers and builders to think outside of standard squares and rectangles.

What difficulties might this building's shape pose when trying to develop the space?

The medical clinic format makes it easier for patients to be seen quickly and by a doctor specializing in the care they need.

It wasn't until 1865 that the half-acre plot saw an actual building. The first on its soil was the German Evangelical Church, which served its **congregation** from 1865 until 1921, when it outgrew the space. Its steeple was removed and sanctuary renovated so that it could function as offices. It did so for just 2 brief years. After that, a neighborhood doctor with a growing medical practice purchased the building and turned it into a thriving clinic staffed by doctors, nurses, lab technicians, and bookkeepers.

A Pioneering Site in Medical Practice

The third use for this Madison plot was as home to one of America's first medical clinics. In the early 1900s, doctors generally worked alone. This changed with the "clinic" model, in which physicians with different areas of expertise came together to form a practice. Clinics hosted the latest and greatest in medical technology, from **anesthetics** *to x-ray machines. The pioneering, family-run Jackson Clinic operated on Hamilton Street until a 1929 fire forced its relocation.*

In 1929, a fire destroyed the clinic. After that, a portion of the lot was sold to retailer Montgomery Ward. This company, which offered something for everyone, was moving from the catalog business to physical stores. With 42,000-plus mail-order customers in the Madison area, the chain designed a four-story **art deco**, **flatiron** building to suit the shape of the lot. It opened in December 1929 and welcomed more than 25,000 people on its first day of operations. For more than 12 years, shoppers scoured its basement for bargains and its upper floors for the latest styles and toys. But more space was needed. In 1942, it shuttered its doors.

The idea of the department store was founded in Paris in 1852. The stores were successful in the United States during the 20th century.

Waiting for the Wish Book

Ice skates. Croquet sets. "Carpetings of Regal Splendor." "Warm Well-Made Horse Blankets Priced Low." The Montgomery Ward mail-order catalog of the late 1800s and early 1900s promised something for everyone. Customers called the massive, 1,000-plus-page catalog the Wish Book. It weighed in at over 4 pounds (2 kilograms) and was sent to more than 2 million homes. It wasn't just a moneymaker for Montgomery Ward. By 1892, it provided more than one-third of the revenues of the United States Post Office.

People didn't just use the Wish Book for shopping. Teachers in rural, one-room schoolhouses used it to teach math, vocabulary, and spelling. And their students? You can be sure that they studied the toy section with avid attention.

During World War II, many young people were fighting overseas and did not have a chance to go to a formal university.

It wasn't empty for long. Eighteen months later, the U.S. Armed Forces moved in. Here—during the peak years of World War II—a movement for adult education was launched. It supported service people pursuing higher learning while **deployed**. During the war years, the United States Armed Forces Institute (USAFI) educated 425,000 students per year through distance education. Students received assignments by mail, which they completed and sent back to professors for review. It was the largest school in the world, and it changed the possibilities for adult learners in America. Here, the General Educational Development exam, or GED exam,

The GED is still a valuable tool for those who aren't able to graduate from a traditional high school for any reason, such as illness, family trauma, relocation, or financial concerns.

None of the building's previous purposes were as exciting as what was coming next.

was developed. This test served as an alternative to a high school diploma, showing that those who passed it possessed knowledge equal to high school graduates across the United States.

In the late 1960s, USAFI moved out. The building was ready for another reinvention. From the early 1970s, it served as an office building for a range of clients. Tenants included government workers, who occupied the space while the nearby capitol underwent renovation. But once that renovation was completed, it waited to be assigned a new purpose by new visionary occupants.

CHAPTER 2

A Museum in Search of a Home

Even before the Madison Children's Museum was established, the folks behind it were masters of working with the materials at hand. In 1979, four area educators—Kay Hendon, Caroline Hoffman, Jeanne Vergeront, and Alan Everhart—started building traveling exhibits. The quartet was driven by the idea that kids learn best through active, **sensory** play and experimentation. With a team of volunteers and an old station wagon, they brought their portable exhibits to local parks, neighborhood centers, and events.

Children's museums are popular all over the country—and the world. Do you have one in your hometown?

The World's First Children's Museum

In the 1890s, the Brooklyn Institute of Arts and Sciences moved to a new home. When it did, it donated cast-off items from its collection to a band of forward-thinking educators. These clever educators used the items as the basis of a museum just for kids. The Brooklyn Children's Museum, the first of its kind, opened in 1899. Today, from Seoul, South Korea, to Stockholm, Sweden, children's museums are a global phenomenon.

American Girl dolls were originally created by Pleasant Company. Today, the brand is owned by Mattel—the same company that sells Barbie.

Calling All Doll Collectors!

Much of the funding for museum expansion came from a unique fundraiser: an auction of American Girl dolls. Starting in the late 1980s, the Pleasant Company donated imperfect and returned merchandise to the Madison Children's Museum. In 1999, the museum hosted a 2-day flash sale with the collected goods. More than 10,000 shoppers from around the country streamed into Madison for the event, which raised over $1 million.

Kids and parents alike loved the interactive pop-up exhibitions. They wanted to enjoy them year-round in a permanent space. The four founders and their volunteers got to work, first taking over the basement of the Wisconsin Academy of Science, Arts, and Letters. This, too, was wildly popular. Soon, more space was needed. They found it in the basement of an old candy factory. Practicing adaptive reuse, they converted it into a museum.

Kay Hendon, Caroline Hoffman, Jeanne Vergeront, and Alan Everhart had grand plans for the new museum space.

The museum called the candy factory home from 1985 until 1991. But with thousands of visitors each year and a growing staff, more space was again needed. So, the team prospected for bigger digs and raised money to support a move. Adaptively reusing yet again, they found space in an old bank with a great view of the state capitol. But within the decade, even more room was needed! They found it just around the corner at 100 North Hamilton.

CHAPTER 3

A Place to Play, Imagine, Dream, and Build

When the Madison Children's Museum acquired its new home in 2005—with the help of a major donation from local **philanthropist** Jerry Frautschi—it wasn't exactly move-in ready. It took 5 years of collaboration between architects, museum staff, exhibition designers, and community members to rework the space into its current form. Architects and contractors worked to address design issues that resulted from a modernization in 1983 to 1984. They restored and preserved original features, like display windows and awnings, lost in the 1980s update. They adapted the floor plan to include all the spaces a children's museum needs: exhibit halls, studios, laboratories, and classrooms. They even added a green roof deck, complete with

The museum's art studio provides a space for Madison's children to make, tinker, play, and create.

chickens, herb and veggie gardens, a rainwater harvesting system, and solar panels.

Meanwhile, museum staff, exhibit designers, and community members—including more than 13,000 children—worked together to create a warm, welcoming environment that reflected Madison and its citizens. Students from three schools helped research the history of an 1830s log cabin that was rebuilt on-site. Thousands of other kids decorated bottle caps with one-of-a-kind illustrations. Each cap became a piece in a series of mosaics that adorn the walls of the art studio. Local artists worked with another 300-plus children to create the ceramic tiles that bring variety and color to the bathrooms.

Artists of the Community, Unite!

In their beloved picture books, author-illustrator Kevin Henkes and illustrator Laura Dronzek celebrate the natural world around us. From the changing seasons to the beauty and variety of bird species, their work has encouraged generations of children to open their eyes to the wonders of planet Earth. Along with more than 100 area artists, the Madison-based couple also left their imprint on the children's museum. A mural that they designed and painted is located just off the main lobby.

Madison-area kids decorated thousands of bottle caps to be used in a mosaic art installation.

Possible-opolis is a creative space created from repurposed materials that inspires kids to be innovative and think creatively in their own lives.

On opening day in 2010, the city's kids walked into the museum knowing the space was theirs—and that they'd already left their marks on it.

Throughout the design process, sustainability guided each and every decision. From the choice of the site to the selection of materials for exhibits, the impact on the Earth was always considered. The second floor's Possible-opolis was created out of 90 percent repurposed and recycled materials. This includes the Hodge Podge Mahal, a crazy climbing structure that counts among its parts a buoy from Lake Michigan and an antique car from Argentina.

Possible-opolis's wooden floor was lifted from a school gym slated for demolition some 80 miles (129 kilometers) away in Milwaukee. Benches were crafted by University of Wisconsin graduate students from the building's **salvaged** wood and metal pieces.

Today, the museum continues to adapt, grow, change, and evolve. But in its walls, floorboards, and exhibits, scraps of the past live on, finding new form and being given new meaning.

A LEED-er in Green Design

In 2014, the Madison Children's Museum earned LEED (Leadership in Energy and Environmental Design) Gold Certification. This certification recognizes the museum as a model of sustainability and green design, making it a leader in the field. Its staffers help other museum professionals explore greening options and rethink their spaces.

Extend Your Learning

Madison Children's Museum staff is fond of historic preservationist Richard Moe's quote: "The greenest building is the one that already exists."

Today, construction and waste are major global issues. Worldwide initiatives—notably the United Nations' 17 **Sustainable Development Goals** (SDGs)—encourage the planet's governments and their citizens to prevent, reduce, recycle, and reuse waste of all varieties (Goal 12). The SDGs also promote the development of clean, environmentally sound, and sustainable infrastructure (Goal 9).

Research this problem and investigate the following questions:

- How much landfill debris comes from demolished buildings in the United States? What is the environmental impact?
- What are the benefits of adaptively reusing buildings that already exist?
- What does the process of adaptive reuse involve? What kind of expertise is needed?
- What are the pros and cons of reusing an existing building? What are the pros and cons of building a new structure?

Survey family members and people in your school community to gauge their awareness of this issue. What can you do to draw further attention to it? Develop a podcast or video—or write an editorial for your local newspaper—that explores the *who*, *what*, *when*, *where*, *why*, and *how* of addressing this challenge.

Glossary

adaptive reuse (uh-DAP-tiv ree-YOOS) reusing a structure for a purpose other than that which it was originally designed to serve

anesthetics (an-is-THET-iks) substances that numb pain

art deco (AHRT DEK-oh) a popular art and architectural style of the 1920s and 1930s

congregation (kahng-grih-GAY-shuhn) a group of people who worship together in a religious setting

correspondence (kor-uh-SPAHN-duhns) written and shared by mail or letter

deployed (dih-PLOYD) sent away to perform a service

flatiron (FLAT-eye-urn) a triangular building shape with one thick end and a narrow, sharp point

illuminated (ih-LOO-muh-nay-tid) illustrated

philanthropist (fuh-LAN-thruh-pist) a person who assists a cause, especially with a donation of money or goods

retail (REE-tayl) the sale of goods (clothes, toys, sporting goods) in a commercial setting

salvaged (SAL-vijd) rescued or saved

sensory (SEN-sur-ee) engaging the five senses (sight, touch, taste, hearing, smell)

Sustainable Development Goals (suhs-STAY-nuh-buhl dih-VEL-uhp-muhnt GOHLZ) 17 goals set by the United Nations, to be achieved by 2030, in order to secure a future that doesn't use up natural resources

yurts (YURTS) circular, domed tents made of material stretched over a framework of crossed wood or metal strips

INDEX